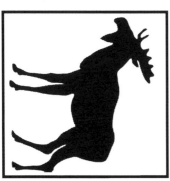
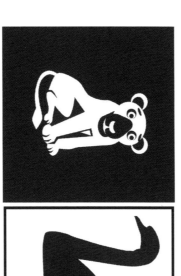
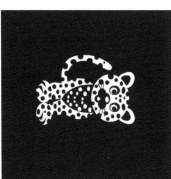
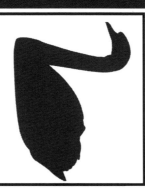
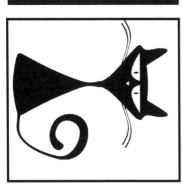
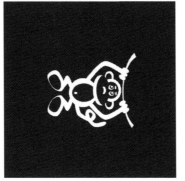

Sample Pages Inside

Printed By CreateSpace

The Best Black and White
Visual Stimulation Book
(Vol 1)
Angelia B. Baron

This Page Is Blank

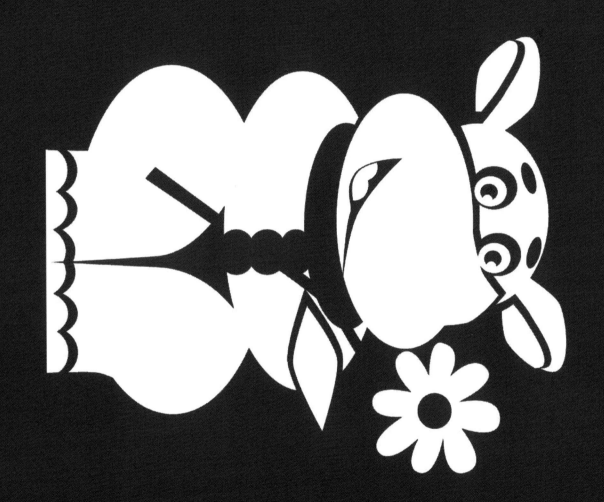

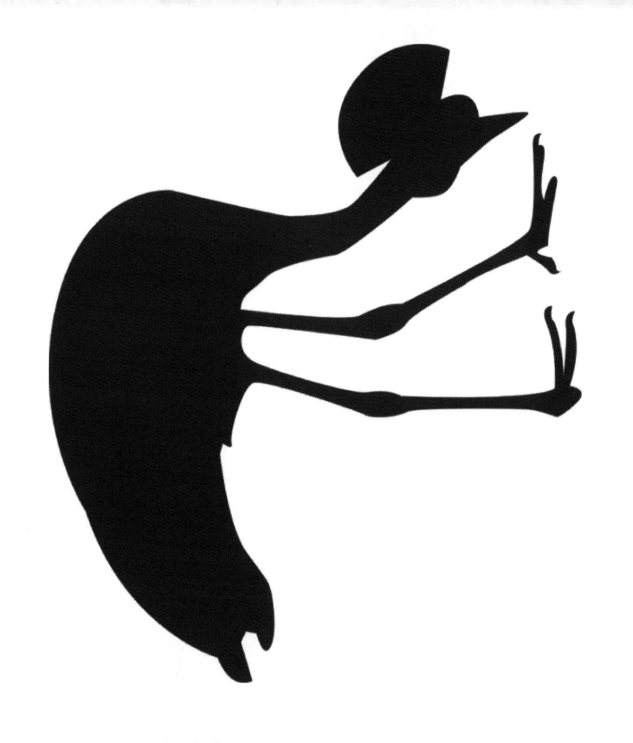

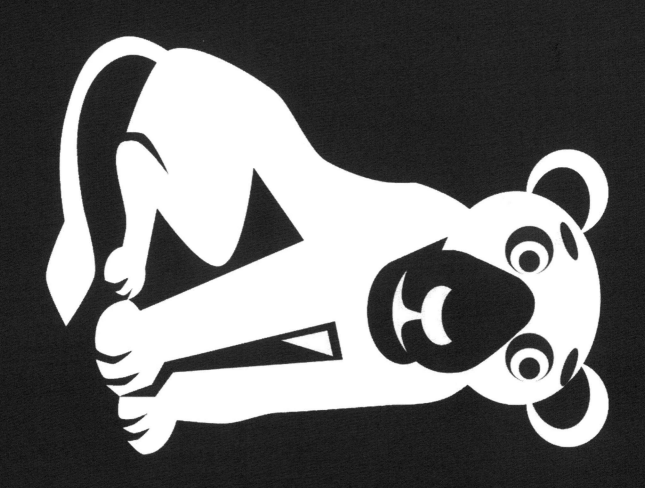

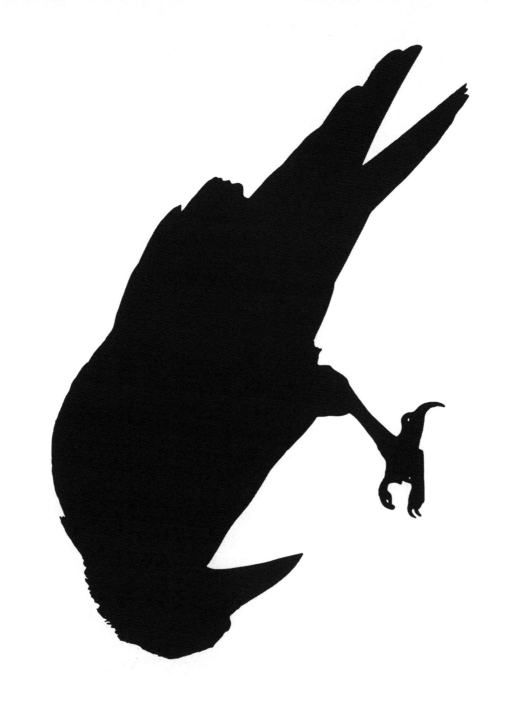

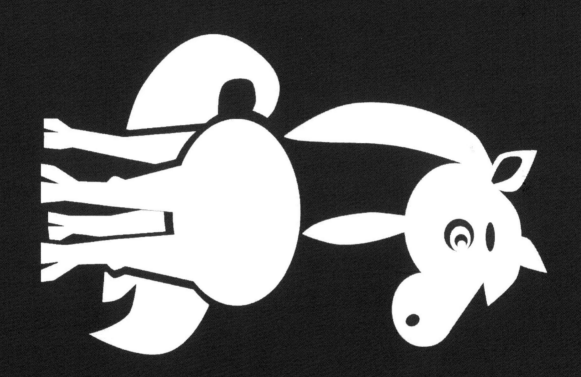

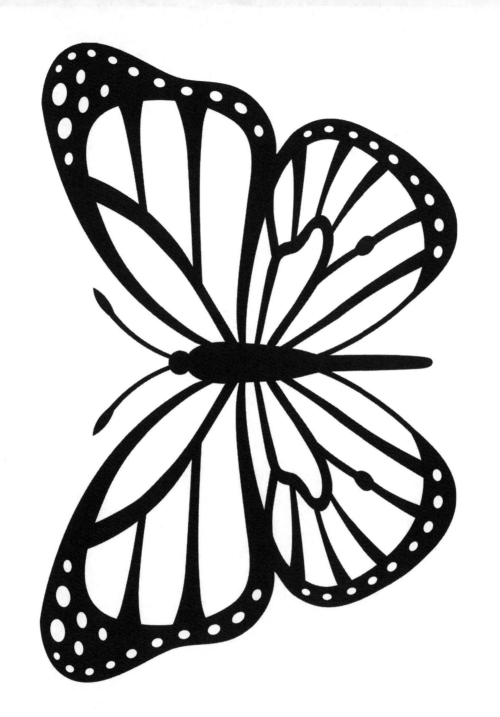

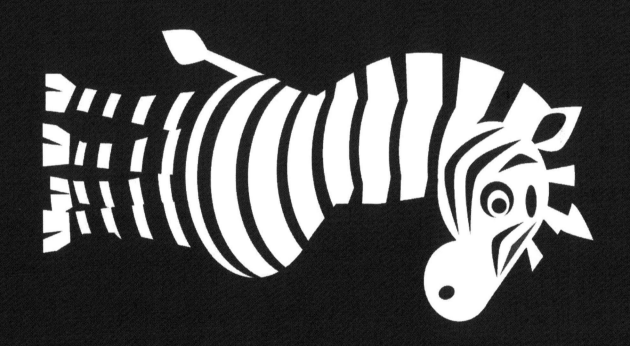

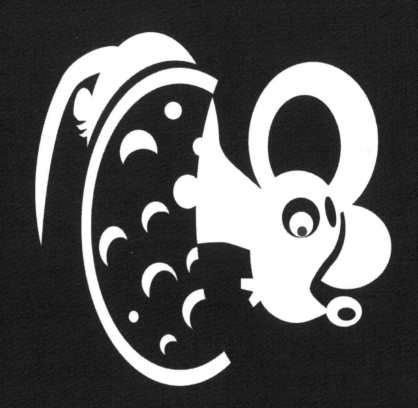

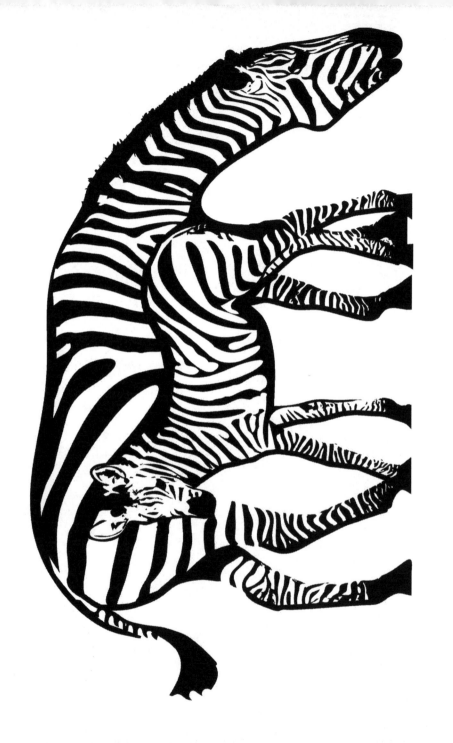

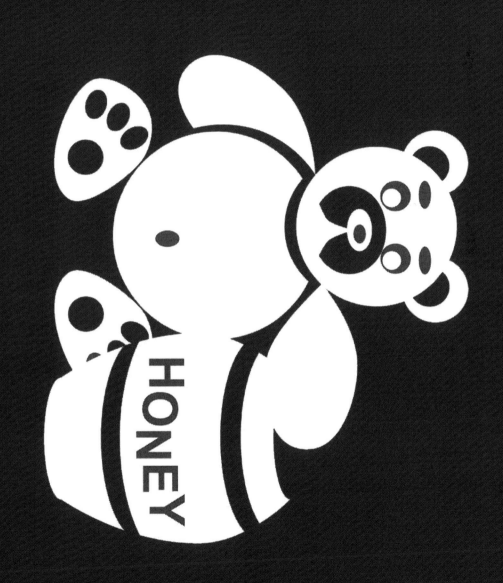

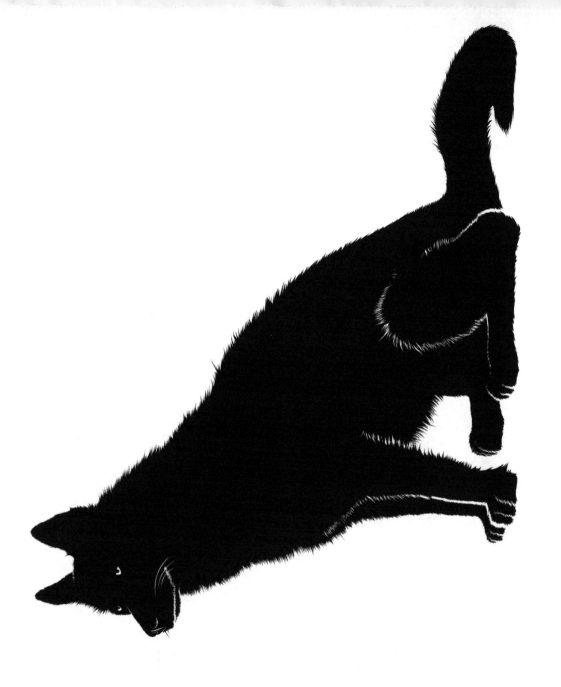

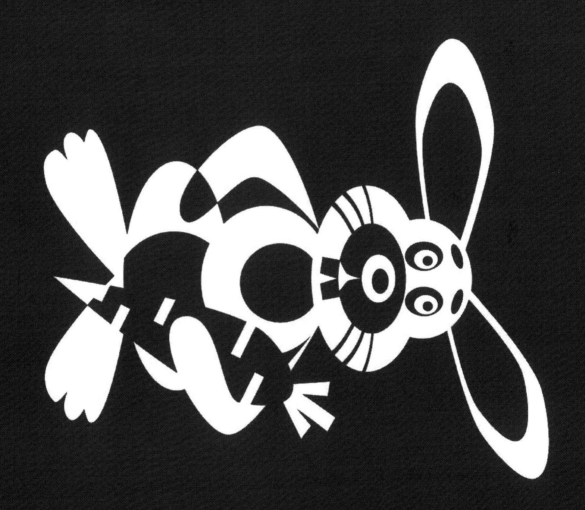

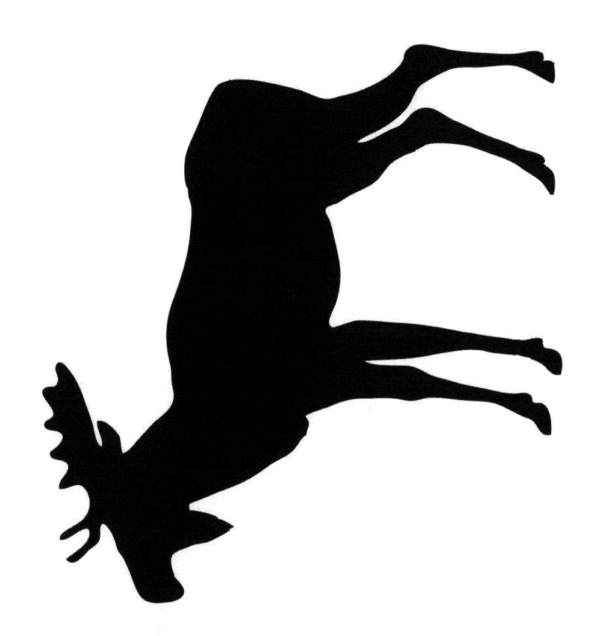

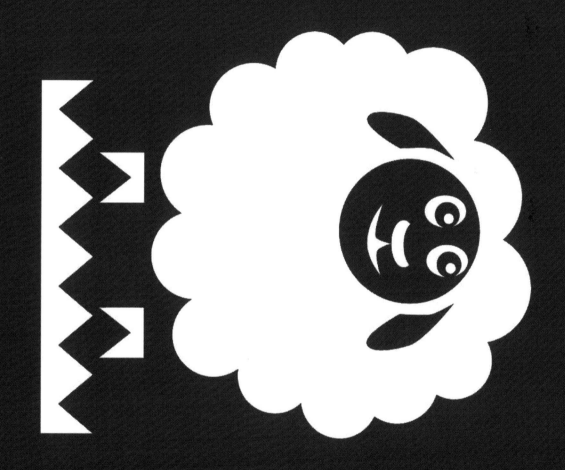

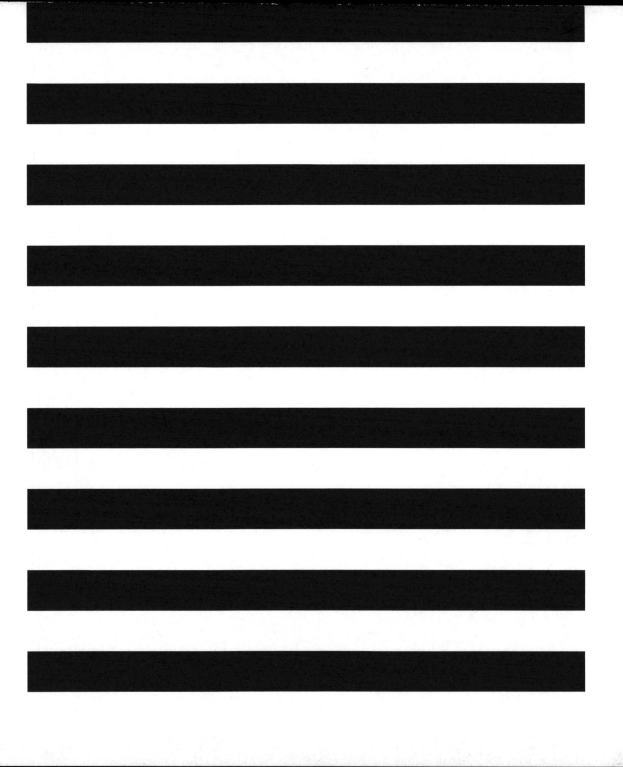

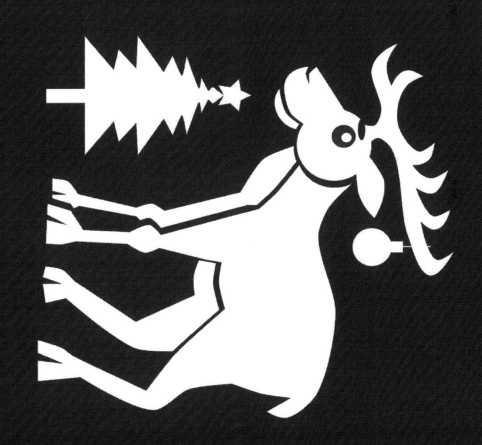

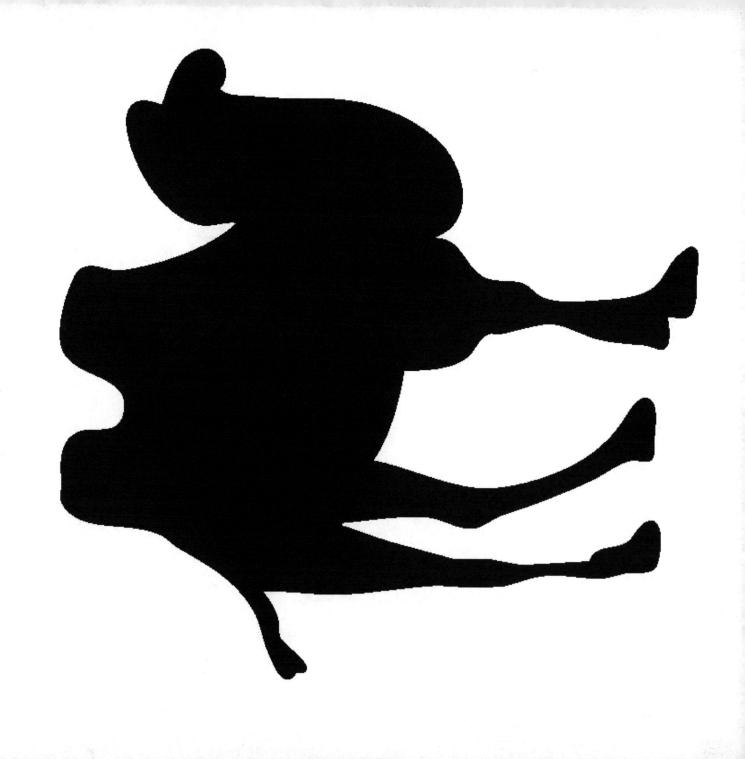

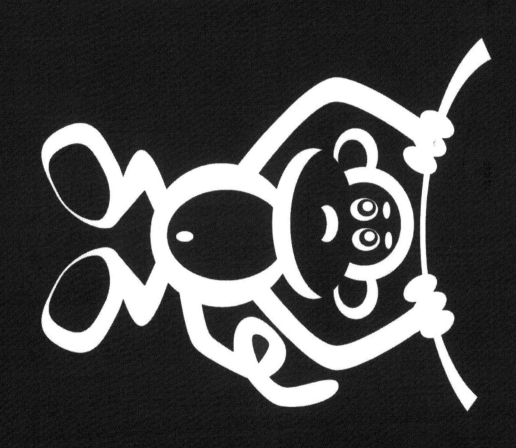

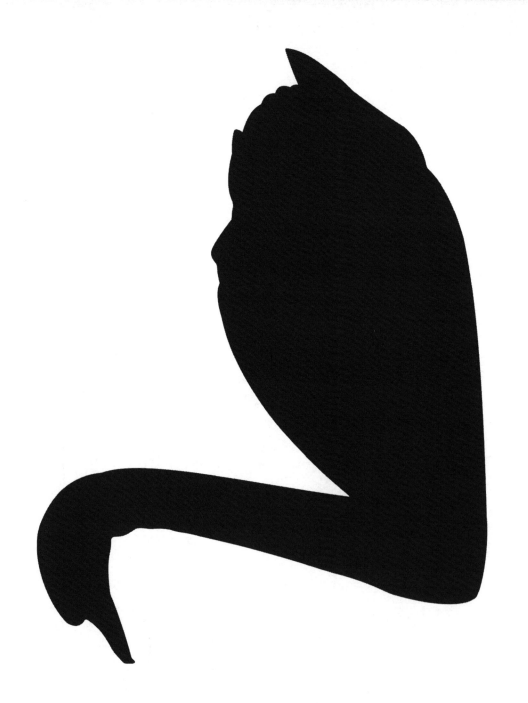

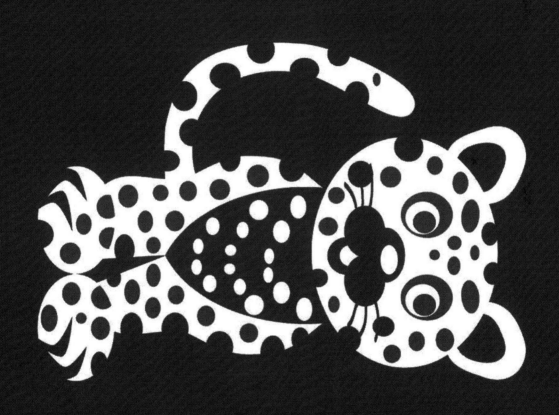

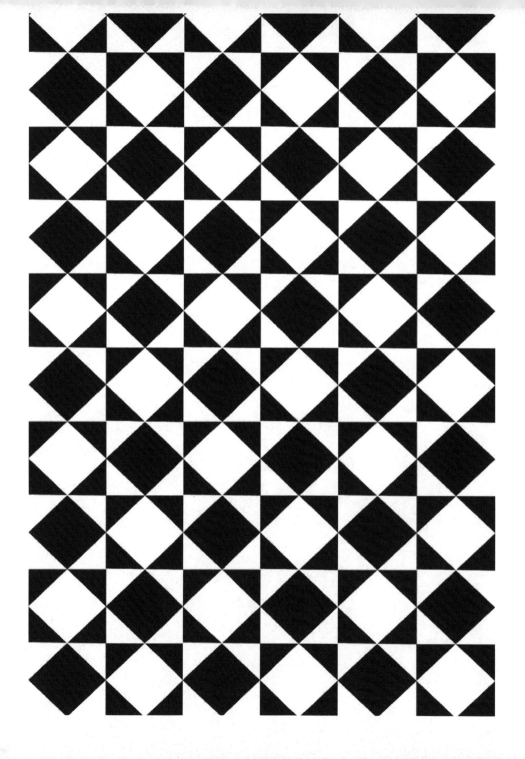

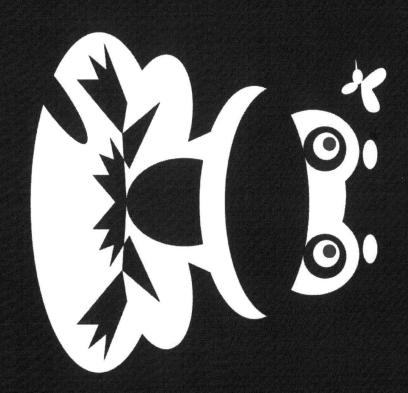

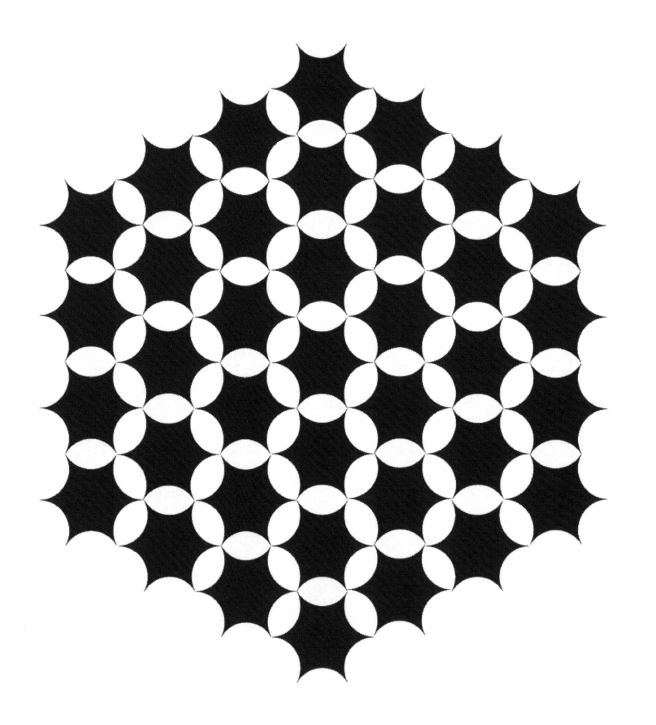

Made in the USA
Las Vegas, NV
02 December 2020

11893852R00015